CW00741998

Metal Detecting the Beach

By Mark Smith

Professional Beach Bum

Copyright 2011 and Beyond
All Rights Reserved

No part of this book may be reproduced, copied, or transmitted in any form without the written consent of the author.

ISBN-13: 978-1482365184
ISBN-10: 1482365189

Table Of Contents

Attention!...3
My First Big Find..5
Metal Detecting Terminology...9
Types of Water Metal Detectors...18
Metal Detector Break Down..21
Copper Ring?...24
Metal Detecting Equipment..29
Proper Etiquette..32
Too Many Quarters?..34
What Can You Find?..36
Creepy Finds?...39
Don't Throw Away Anything..41
Jewelry Marks – Is It Real...46
Selling Your Finds...52
Metal Detecting With Kids...55
Shells On The Beach..56
Research Really Pays Off!..66
The Changing Tides...68
Can you really find rings on the beach?......................................71
The Weather Can Wreak Havoc On The Beach............................73
The Seasons...74
A Big Ring and A UFO..78
Reading The Beach..82
How To Hunt...87
Pinpointing A Target..100
Digging Up Your Targets..102
Hunting In The Water 104
One Final Story..106

Attention!

Before you grab your metal detector and head to the beach, make sure that you are allowed to use a metal detector on the beach. There are some areas where you can't use a metal detector on the beach or in the water. You can't use a metal detector on federal land, and in Florida, state parks are off limits.

Some of the images in this book have been printed sideways or in landscape format. This is allows for larger images with more detail. When you find an image like this, just turn your book sideways for the best viewing experience.

Turn book sideways

My First Big Find

I remember my first "Big" find like it was yesterday. I was still very new to metal detecting on the beach, but I had a good idea, or at least I thought I had a good idea of where to look.

The particular beach that I was hunting was undergoing a beach renourishment project. This is where they pump in loads of sand from somewhere else to replace sand that has previously eroded from storms. They were using dredging equipment to get the sand from one location to another. In all of the dredged sand, I was finding small pieces of aluminum. This is commonly referred to as "can slaw." When the dredging machine sucks up sand, they also suck up any garbage with it. This meant that all of the old aluminum cans were getting sucked up by the dredging equipment. They were literally pouring sand that was full of garbage all over the beach, but they obviously did not care. This made hunting on this particular beach very difficult.

I decided to move down the beach as far away from the dredging as I possibly could. The beach that I was hunting on was a stretch of beach that was about 7 miles long. The sand was being pumped onto about 5 miles of beach, that left me with two miles of good clean beach to hunt.

Once I got to the clean section of beach, I started finding

targets immediately. I was finding a lot of modern clad coins. Nothing worth noting, but at least it was keeping me busy. I decided to move away from the water and try my luck closer to the dunes. I have never had much luck in this area, but it never hurts to try something new.

A tropical storm had recently brushed the coast and created some big seas that had eroded a large section of dunes. This looked like a great place to hunt.

Eagerly I took my metal detector to this area. At the time I was using a PI metal detector. The letters PI stand for pulse induction. This type of metal detector has no discrimination. It picks up everything. I would regularly find bobby pins, staples, bbs, and all sorts of other types of junk with this machine, but it went deep, and it was the only machine that I had at the time.

Once I got to the section of eroded dunes, I started getting signals all over the place. I could see where what looked like a huge set of waves had come in and destroyed this section of dunes. I could also see what looked like an area where the waves settled and dumped whatever they were carrying with them. All of the lighter material had been taken out with the tide.

My first target was a large 3 ounce pyramid sinker. Just a few inches from that was another, and then another. This area was loaded with lead sinkers, and I was happily digging them up. Sometimes two or three at a time in my scoop.

I had carved out a big area of sand, and I had well over a few pounds of lead sinkers in my pockets. I had so many that my pants kept coming down. You might be asking yourself why I would keep all of the weights. I keep everything that I find. That is one of the cool things about metal detecting on the beach. You help clean things up.

Lead is a heavy metal, and you will often find other heavy metals close by, so I kept digging up all of these lead weights hoping to find a piece of gold or two, but I found something even better.

It was hot. I was sweating, and my pants were overloaded with lead weights. I must have been a sight to everyone on the beach as I frantically dug up lead.

By this time I was getting tired. I looked in my scoop and there was what looked like a large ring laying in the bottom, but it was not gold. It looked like lead or pewter. I had no idea what it was, and it was the first ring that I had found on the beach.

I was excited to find a ring. I reached in my scoop and pulled it out. The ring was huge, and it was very heavy. It had to have been a mans ring, and he must have been a giant. I held the ring up to the sunlight. Man was it ugly. I could see some writing on the inside of the ring. There was an inscription that read "Hercules." I could barely make out some other writing on the ring as well. It said, "950 Plat." At the time I had no idea what this meant, and out of frustration, I almost threw this big ugly ring as far as I could, but I threw it in my pocket with all of the weights and called it the day.

When I got home and did a little research, I learned that 950 Plat meant that the ring was PLATINUM! The very first ring that I found on the beach was made of one of the most expensive metals on our planet. I was now hooked on metal detecting. I could not believe that I found this huge, heavy and very valuable platinum ring with my metal detector.

Metal Detecting Terminology

It seems that everything has its own unique language, even metal detecting. If you are new to metal detecting then you may not be familiar with some of the terms that I am going to be using throughout this book. This section will help you learn the metal detecting lingo.

Sanded In: This is when there is an over abundance of sand built up on the beach. All of the targets are buried beyond the reach of your metal detector. Unfortunately this happens a lot, and when the beach is sanded in, you are better off hunting somewhere else. Here s a good example picture.

Notice the nice flat beach. This is what a sanded in beach looks like.

The Dry: The dry is anywhere on the beach that the water has not hit in either a long time or ever. Hunting the dry can be fun, and you can find some great treasure here. I also find more trash here than anywhere else. The dunes would be a very good example.

The Parking Lot: This is not a literal parking lot, and not every beach has what I like to call "The Parking Lot." Only beaches that allow you to drive and park your car on them have parking lots, and as you can guess, this is the area where everyone parks. You can find it in **The Dry.**

The Wet: Ahh, the opposite of the dry. The wet is the area of sand that is exposed during low tide. The sand itself is wet, and during high tide it is under water. At certain times of the year, this area of beach can be the most productive for gold. Do not miss it. This is where I like to spend most of my time metal detecting the beach, unless something else catches my eye.

Certain metal detectors do not function well here. The salt just makes them go wild. Metal detectors that are made for use in the salt water will have no problems here.

The Water Line: This one is self explanatory. This is the area of beach where the water meets the sand. The water line is always productive at low tide, and if it is not, then you can always take a few steps towards the wet.

The Towel Line: This is an area of beach where everyone puts down their towels and lays out in the sun. This area can be part of the wet or the dry, and it should never be overlooked, especially if no where else on the beach is producing any treasures.

Coin Line: A coin line is a great thing to find and a wonder of physics. A coin line is a line of coins that runs straight and parallel to the beach. It is usually found in the wet. If you find a coin line, work it hard because where there are lots of coins, you just might find jewelry.

Sticky Spot: This is my personal favorite. This is a spot on the beach that defies all logic. In a sticky spot you will find lots of goodies in a random pattern. They will not be evenly distributed in a line. It's more like some giant hand from the sky reached down and threw them onto the beach. These sticky spots can be as small as a beach chair, or as large as a house. Sticky spots are where I find the coolest things.

Cuts: Cuts are formed when the ocean removes a large amount of sand from the front of the beach. If you are on a beach that is cutting, or one that has been recently cut by eroding winds and weather you will know it. Cuts are small cliffs that have formed due to the absence of sand. They can be as high as 20 feet, or as low as a few inches. If there are large cuts on the beach, then you will have a very good chance of finding some treasure.

This picture shows you a good example of a nice 3 foot cut.

This picture was taken with my back facing the water. A

lot of sand had been removed by a simple change in the weather.

On the next page you will see a good example of a huge cut that was caused by hurricane Sandy in 2012. In this situation, the hurricane was hundreds of miles away from this particular location and it still did that much damage!

Metal Detecting Terminology

Scallops: Scallops are a lot like cuts, but they may not be so obvious, and if you are new to metal detecting you may not even notice them. The best way to identify a scalloped area of beach is to stand and look parallel to the water.

For example: If your beach runs North and South, then the water will either be on your East or your West. If you stand in the middle of the beach at low tide, and look either North or South, you will be able to see scallops if the exist. They can be very long and shallow, or short and deep. Either type of scallop is a great place to start hunting. You won't be able to see the longer and shallower scallops when you get in them, but from a distance you should have no problems seeing them. There is a good example on the next page.

If you look hard enough, you can see a scalloped area on the beach in the distance.

This is a shallow and very long scallop. It can be deceiving trying to determine distance on a beach, but this scallop is really long.

Types of Water Metal Detectors

Luckily when it comes to beach metal detectors there are not that many different types. There are plenty of different brands, makes and models, but only a few different types. Choosing which one is right for you may take some trial and error. You may or may not need a machine that is actually waterproof. If you plan on hunting in the water, then of course you will need a waterproof machine. If you just plan on hunting the area of beach that gets exposed during low tide, you may not need to get a water proof machine.

PI or Pulse Induction Machine – This was my first waterproof detector. A PI machine uses no discrimination. It will make a sound on anything that is made of metal, or has metal in it. These can be great if you are hunting a beach that has some serious treasure history. If you are looking for modern dropped jewelry, then a PI machine may be overkill. In my case, it was overkill.

This metal detector would pick up anything. I was digging up bobby pins, tools, staples, bullets, and tent stakes. These types of machines work great, but while you are busy digging up all of that junk, someone else is digging up the gold.

I noticed this when other metal detectorists were passing me by. I was even approached by a fellow with a different type of machine, and when I explained to him how my machine worked, and I then showed him my pocket full of junk, he looked at me and said one word, "Why?"

I decided to change my metal detector to a different type. I wanted a VLF machine.

VLF Machines – VLF stands for very low frequency. The good thing about these types of machines is the fact that they allow you to discriminate out certain types of metals. I was only looking to discriminate out iron objects. I am willing to dig up everything else. There are a lot of people who argue back and forth which machine is better. The answer is simple though. The better machine is the one that works best for you.

Some people will say that if there is a piece of gold underneath a piece of iron, then you will be passing it up with a VLF machine. I have found this to be entirely untrue. I have found gold rings that were right next to and underneath pieces of iron with my machine. It took me a while to learn how to do this, but the more I used my machine, the better I became at understanding what it was trying to tell me.

Dual or 2 Box Metal Detectors – These are serious business. They use two coils or boxes to search the ground, and they can find items as deep as five or more feet. You will not see very many of these on the beach, but the hardcore treasure hunters use them.

So here is a quick re-cap of the different types of machines and the pros and cons.

PI Machine – *No discrimination. You will have to dig up everything.*

VLF Machine – *Can discriminate out certain metals, but when you use discrimination, you may be passing up good stuff.*

Dual Box Machines – *These are for the serious hunters out there. They can detect metal objects very deep. Deeper than most of us are willing to dig.*

Metal Detector Break Down

Metal detectors do break down from time to time, but that is not what this chapter is about. If you are already familiar with metal detectors then skip ahead to the next chapter. This chapter was designed to help people who are just getting into the hobby.

Just about every metal detector is built the same. There are some exceptions, but the most common beach hunting metal detectors are made up of 5-7 parts. The coil, the shaft, the arm cuff, the controls, the power source, the display and the headphones. Let's start at the bottom and work our way to the top of the metal detector.

The Coil – The coil is the round part at the end of the metal detector. It is the part that you scan the ground with.

Every single metal detector uses a coil. Some are different shapes, and some are bigger than others, but bigger does not always mean better. A bigger coil may let you cover a wider area with every sweep, but in my personal experience, larger coils compromise depth.

My machine uses a standard ten inch coil. It is ten inches in diameter. At one point, I purchased an aftermarket 15 inch coil and put it on my machine. In my opinion this larger coil was not nearly as sensitive, and it lacked much of the depth that my stock coil had. I ended up removing the larger coil and selling it to a friend.

The Shaft – The shaft is the long metal rod that holds everything together. This is one instance when having a longer shaft really makes a difference. You can cover more ground with each swing with a longer shaft. It sounds funny when you think about it, but it is true.

The Arm Cuff – This is where your arm rests while you swing your metal detector. It should be comfortable. These can be changed as well. Mine broke, and I just replaced it with a section of PVC pipe. Thanks to my friend Will Rogers for this tip.

The Controls – This is the part of your metal detector that lets you make adjustments to how it works. They are all different so I won't go over any specifics other than experiment with it to get the best results. What works for me might not work for you and vice versa.

The Power Source – All metal detectors will require some sort of power. Some will take batteries which is a pain, but others will come with a rechargeable battery pack. Here is a tip for you. **Always carry a second set of batteries, or a second battery pack with you every time you hunt.**

The Display – Some metal detectors have visual displays that will help you ID a target before you dig it up. I have never used a machine with a display. I like to use my ears.

The Headphones – This is the most important part of your metal detector. This is how your metal detector will talk to you. Each machine is different, and certain items will make certain tones. It is up to you to learn what these tones mean. In time the difference in tones can tell you what an item is before you dig it up.

Copper Ring?

One of the greatest things about metal detecting the beaches is that you will never know what you will find or when. As you become a more experienced hunter, you will be able to determine if a spot looks good, but unless you have x-ray vision you will never know exactly what lies beneath the sand.

Here is a story about one of my best finds.

The weather was normal. The ocean was calm, but for some reason the tides had cut a very deep slough that ran parallel to the water. This slough was at least 3 feet deep and I was finding a lot of quarters on the high tide side of the trough. Here is an aerial view.

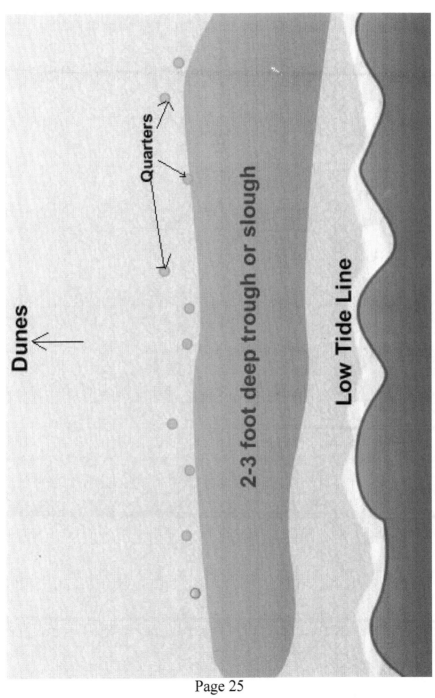

My past experience had taught me that quarters were a good thing. The quarters that were turning up were green.

This told me that they had been there for a while. About 1 hour into the hunt, I got a really good signal mixed in with the quarters. I looked in my scoop and saw what looked like a copper colored ring laying in the bottom.

It was the middle of Summer and there were a lot of people around so I quietly deposited the ring into my pocket. You have to be careful hunting around people. There are a lot of very dishonest people out there who will try to take the things that you find as theirs. **The worst**

thing that you can do is jump up and down when you have a good find. It can be really hard trying to act natural when there is a good target in the bottom of your scoop.

I kept following this line knowing that this big copper colored ring was just rolling around in my pocket. It was burning a hole in my pocket, but there were still too many people around to really check this thing out.

I decided to turn and go back towards my car. The suspense of what I had found was killing me. I picked up the pace and got back to my car. I put my gear away, reached into my pocket and took out the copper ring. I rolled it around in my hand. Boy it was really heavy. I tried to see if there were any markings on the inside of the ring, but I had been in the sun all day, and my eyes were not picking up the small writing on the inside of the ring. I would have to wait until I got home and hand it over to my wife who has the eagle eye.

I showed my wife and she looked at the inside of the ring and said it says "595." I asked her if she was sure, and she said, "Yep." That didn't make any sense at all. There are no ring markings that say 595. I cleaned the ring under some running water and rubbed the inside of the band where the writing was. I handed it to her again and asked her to look again. This time she said, "Oh! It says 585." That means it is 14kt gold, but why did it look like copper? It was 14kt rose gold, and it was thick and heavy. This one ring weighed just under one ounce on my scale!

14kt gold is a little over 50% pure gold and at just under an ounce this turned out the be a really good find.

Metal Detecting Equipment

In order to make the most of your metal detecting, you are going to need to get some additional equipment. Your metal detector will only help you find the treasure. It is up to you to retrieve it, and without the proper equipment you will never be able to get your buried treasure.

Beach Scoops - Your first thought might be this. "I can just use a shovel." You can do that if you want, but there are specialized shovels called beach scoops that will put an ordinary shovel to shame. I can't say enough about how important a good scoop is. It is by far the most important piece of metal detecting equipment that you will own next to your metal detector. You will be breaking your back without a proper beach scoop.

I learned this lesson the hard way. When I first started metal detecting on the beach, I thought I knew it all, and I did not want to spend a bunch of money on a scoop. I did not mind spending money on a metal detector, but why should I spend $100 or more on a scoop? I invested about $25.00 for a little metal hand held scoop. It worked. It made my back hurt. It took three times as long to retrieve a target and it was almost impossible to retrieve an item that was underwater without a scuba tank, but other than that it worked just fine. Of course I quickly saw the error in my judgment, and I knew that I had to get a long handled scoop.

People will argue all day long about which scoop is best. I am not going to get into that. I will tell you what has worked best for me over the years.

I use a stainless steel scoop that is handmade by a guy in Florida. It has a lightweight fiberglass handle, and a stainless steel diamond head scoop. It has worked for me flawlessly throughout the years. I have even actually spoken with the fellow that makes them. He is a great guy that stands behind his products 100%.

They are not the cheapest scoops on the market, but mine has been worth every single penny. I don't have to bend over to dig or retrieve anything. It cuts through the sand like a hot knife through butter. It works great in the water, and it will also allow you to sift through everything and just leave the goodies behind. You can find these scoops on this website: http://www.nuttallenterprises.com/

I will say it again. **Get the best scoop that you can afford**. It will help you more than you may think.

Pouch - I don't use a finds pouch, but a lot of other people do. I just throw everything in my pockets. If I find a really good item, I may wear it until I get back to my car.

Backpack - I used to wear a backpack while I hunted the beach. I don't anymore. It got too hot, and I am never all that far from my car. If you are going to be hunting a beach where you will be far from your car, then a backpack will be essential.

Waterproof Cell Phone Case – I just recently started using one of these and I am glad that I did. You never know when it may rain, or a big wave will come rolling in and soak you. These little waterproof cell phone cases are really cheap, and they keep your phone dry.

Sunscreen – I should not have to warn you about the dangers of over exposure to the sun. Make sure that you put on some sunscreen if you are going to be hunting the beach for any extended periods of time.

Sunglasses – A good pair of polarized sunglasses will keep the sun out of your eyes, and the glare off the water. I never hunt without mine.

Food and Water – You may not think that metal detecting is tiring, but after you spend a few hours in the sun and dig around 50 holes, your energy levels will drop. Always make sure that you have plenty of good high octane food, and plenty of water to keep you nice and hydrated.

Proper Etiquette

There are a few unspoken rules to metal detecting on the beaches, but not every metal detectorist follows them. If you are going out to hunt the beach, keep these rules in mind.

Fill In Your Holes – This unspoken rule is the one that most people ignore. It is just common courtesy to fill in all of your holes. If you are digging in waist deep or even deeper water, then you won't have to worry about it, but if you are digging holes out of the water, always fill them in.

Take All Of Your Finds – You will dig up a lot of trash. Don't be a jerk and put it back in the sand. Take it with you. I have seen plenty of metal detectorists dig holes, retrieve a piece of trash and then throw it back in the hole and leave the hole uncovered. Don't do this. I have found that the beach will reward you with nice things if you remove all of the trash that you dig up.

Don't Steal People's Spots – If you go to a beach to detect, and you see someone else is already there, don't get in front of them and start hunting where they are about to go. I have seen countless people do this, and it has made me want to throw some of the lead weights in my pocket at them, but I just turn and go back the other way. There is plenty of beach to hunt. There is no reason to move in on another person's hunt. If you see someone going one way, do the right thing and go the opposite way.

There is nothing wrong with approaching another person that is detecting to say hi, or ask how they are doing, but turn your machine off before you do. Two machines together will not play nice, and as you get closer to the other machine, you will be causing all sorts of interference.

Too Many Quarters?

I like digging up quarters. I can never have too many. One day I was hunting a new spot. I had been there in the past, but it had been about a year since I had been there.

This place was not your typical beach. It was along the inter-coastal waterway. You can still find plenty of treasure there too. Where ever people are or have been, you will find treasure.

In this particular place they had recently done some dredging in a nearby channel. I was finding older items that must have been stirred up as part of the dredging. I found two Mecury Dimes side by side, and then I found a really old rust encrusted pocket knife. My next target was another really old rust encrusted pocket knife. It was strange how things were in small groups.

I was about waist deep in the water when my coil went over and area, and it went nuts. There were targets every couple of inches. I dug in with my scoop, rinsed the sand away and saw two quarters sitting in the bottom of my scoop. Hey! 50 cents! I like that, but there were more targets in the same small area. My next scoop of sand revealed three quarters in one scoop, but there were still more targets in the same hole. I scooped again, rinsed away the sand and this time there were four quarters sitting in the bottom of my scoop, and there were still more targets to dig.

By the time I was done, I had recovered over 100 quarters from an area no bigger than a coffee table. They were everywhere. I had so many of them that I had to stop hunting because the weight of all the quarters was pulling down my pants. You never know what you are going to find, and I have never had another episode like that. All of those quarters must have been there from the backwash of the dredging, or I had discovered someone's cache. Either way I was happy to dig up that many quarters in one small spot.

What Can You Find?

The question should be more along the lines of what can't you find. Using a metal detector on the beach will uncover all kinds of surprises. Most of us are there looking for some old pirates treasure, or some modern gold that has been lost, but you will find everything else as well.

Coins – I have found every type of American coin that there is, and of course I have found more pennies than anything else. I have also found plenty of foreign coins that I could not recognize.

Coins will make up the bulk of your finds on the beach. Most of them never look that good either. I just throw them all in a bucket when I get home. At the end of the year, I will go through them and see if I have enough change to take a nice vacation, and I usually do!

There are even some beaches that are known to cough up old Spanish coins.

Trash – You will find your fair share of trash too. Once you start metal detecting on the beaches, you will be amazed at what is laying just a few inches under the sand.

Cell Phones – I have found some of the best highest dollar cell phones that money can buy, and not one of them has ever been in working condition. The little memory cards that were in them were salvageable though.

Teeth – You read that right. I have actually found teeth. These were human teeth that had gold fillings. I have also found complete gold bridges. There is nothing quite like looking in the bottom of your scoop and seeing human teeth. Here is a picture of a gold filling I found. Nice huh?

Jewelry – This is what you want to see laying in the bottom of your scoop. I have found every type of jewelry imaginable. I have found bracelets, rings, necklaces, earrings, and plenty of other types of rings that went into some odd piercings. I have found both modern jewelry and some very old jewelry. The funny thing about jewelry in the sea is this. Gold will not tarnish. It looks just as good coming out as it did the day it went in. Silver on the other hand turns an awful shade of black. It is best to leave any old coins in the state they were when you found them. If you don't know what you are doing, cleaning them may cause some irreversible damage.

Creepy Finds?

I have also had a few creepy finds. One in particular stands out in my memory. It was Winter in Florida. It does not get that cold, but a freak cold front had come through and parked right on top of the state.

Not only did this cold front make from some rather terrible metal detecting, but a lot of the local fish that migrate out of the area were caught off guard too. In this instance, the cold front killed quite a lot of fish.

I was hunting on the beach that morning and there were dead fish everywhere. I have never seen so many dead and dying fish. I saw one Snook that was easily a record breaker laying on the beach. I was surrounded by all of these dead fish when suddenly I got a very low tone on my metal detector.

I had never heard a tone this low before. It peaked my interest. I dug the target and can you guess what was in the bottom of my scoop? It was a crematory tag that came from someone's ashes being dumped at sea. Here I was, surrounded by all of these dead fish and I find this? I said a quick prayer, and threw the crematory tag back out into the water.

A few miles down the beach, I spotted this dead fish. It just made the day even more bizarre. It is an Ocean Sunfish.

Creepy Finds?

Don't Throw Away Anything

It may seem like junk at first, but you should never ever throw anything away that you find unless you are 100% positive that it is garbage. There are instances of people throwing away old Spanish coins because they just looked like large black metal discs. A quick flick of the wrist, and those 300 year old coins skip right across the water where they quickly sink to the bottom waiting to be found by someone with a little more experience. It may be an object of mystery now, but in the future you may be able to figure out exactly what it is. I have the perfect example.

I was hunting a section of beach during the early morning hours. The beach that I was hunting allows driving. People drive up and down the beach all day long. The night before, there was a huge Mardis Gras parade that went down the beach. There were thousands of people everywhere. Now you know why I wanted to hunt the area the next morning.

A large crowd of partying people leave one thing behind, and they leave it behind in huge numbers. Trash. It was everywhere. It was rather disgusting actually. Empty beer bottles and cans right next to garbage cans.

I was finding plenty of bottle tops, pull tabs, and other miscellaneous pieces of garbage. It was hard work, but I was cleaning up the beach, and the beach likes to reward you every once in a while. I got a good low tone on my metal detector. It was right in the middle of a tire track, and it was a shallow target.

I was hunting the dry. I quickly sifted the sand through my scoop, and in the bottom of my scoop was a smashed ring. At least I thought it was a ring. It must have been some cheap costume jewelry from the Mardis Gras parade. I put it in my pocket and went on hunting. Here is a picture of the smashed ring.

When I got home, I showed the crushed ring to my wife, and she said the same thing. "It looks like costume jewelry from the parade. I tossed it in my pile of junk jewelry that I kept in an old tackle box, and completely forgot about it.

At the time I had no idea how to acid test a piece of jewelry, so that smashed ring sat in my tackle box for over a year.

A year passed and in that year, I learned a lot about how to identify jewelry. I had purchased an acid test and a jewelers loupe, and I had become very good at Iding my finds.

I got back from a recent hunt where I found some junk jewelry. I tossed my new junk jewelry into my pile that was growing in my tackle box, and that smashed ring bounced to the top of the pile. I had completely forgotten about it. I realized that I had never looked at it with a loupe or anything.

I quickly grabbed the smashed ring from the pile and looked at it with my loupe. A large part of the band was missing, and there were no markings. I showed it to my wife and told her to take a look. She looked at it, and then she flipped it around and looked at all of the stones on the front. Then she says this to me, "The top of this ring is all smashed and broken, but the stones don't have a scratch on them. Do you think they could be real diamonds?" The thought had never crossed my mind. It was just costume jewelry.

I wanted to try a diamond test that I had learned about. Sometimes, not all of the times, a diamond will glow a milky white if you put it under a black light. My son had a black light in his room. I flipped the light on, and three of the stones had that Erie glow. I was convinced they were real diamonds which meant that the ring was either white gold or platinum.

I broke out the acid test and it tested as 18k gold. I was thrilled. This ring had quite a few large diamonds in it. I took it to a jeweler to have it looked at. As soon as I handed it to him he tossed it up in the air a few times and said, "This is platinum." He looked at the stones and said, "All of the stones are real, and they are very old. They are a very old style diamond called European Mine cut. This ring is from the early 1900s or even earlier." I was thrilled to say the least. I asked him if he could repair it, and he said "Of Course!" Within a few days it was repaired and on my wife's finger.

When I first found this ring, I had almost thrown it in the garbage. Just think about that for a second. I had an antique platinum diamond ring that had over 2 carats of diamonds in it sitting in my house for over a year, and I had no idea. DON'T THROW ANYTHING AWAY!

Here is a picture of the ring after it was repaired.

Jewelry Marks – Is It Real

One thing that I have learned from all of my metal detecting is how to determine if a piece of jewelry is actually real or not. If you stick at it, you will find plenty of your own jewelry, and you will at times be wondering if some of your finds are real.

The first thing that you need to know is that almost every single piece of real jewelry is marked in one way or another, and I don't mean lover's inscriptions either. These marks can usually be found along the inside band of a ring, the clasp of a necklace, the back of a pendant, or the shaft of an earring.

Some of these markings are tiny, and I had to shell out some cash for a jewelers loupe. This great little tool set me back about five bucks. It is a small magnifying glass that will allow you to quickly ID your finds. I have used it to ID all of my finds, look for mint marks on coins, and get up close and personal with a diamond or two.

Here is a break down of all of the most common jewelry marks and what they mean. Unfortunately there are literally hundreds of marks used in Silver jewelry. I will just cover the most common ones that you will most likely run into.

10k – This means 10 karat gold. It can be white, yellow, or rose. About 40% gold.

10kp – There seems to be some speculation on this one, but every time I have found this, it meant 10 karat plumb, which means exactly 10 karats. About 40% gold.
14k – This means 14 karat gold. It can be white, yellow, or rose and it means that the jewelry contains 58% gold.

14kp – This means that the jewelry is pure 14 karats. About 58% gold.

18k – This means 18 karat gold. It can be white, yellow, or rose. About 75% gold.

20k – This means 20 karat gold. About 83% gold.

22k – This means 22 Karat gold. About 91% Gold

24k – This means 24 karat gold. This is100% pure gold!

.417 – Same as 10k.

.585 – Same as 14k.

.750 – Same as 18k.

.833 – Same as 20k.

.999 – Same as 24k.

PLAT – This means platinum.

PT – This can also mean platinum and can be prefixed, or followed by a number.

900 – This means platinum. It is 90% Platinum.

950 – This also means platinum. It is 95% Platinum.
Stainless Steel – These rings have gained popularity. They are usually marked: Stainless Steel, S.S., or Steel.

Silver- Self Explanatory.

S. Silver – This means Sterling Silver

Sterling Silver – Self Explanatory.

925 – This means the item is silver. About 92.5% pure.

Titanium – These rings are very light.

Tungsten – These are becoming more popular too. Most of the times they are an odd flat black color.

CZ – If you find a ring with a stone in it, this means that the stone is cubic zirconia.

CW – If you find a ring with a stone in it, this could be prefixed or followed by a number. This number would be the amount of total carat weight of the diamond.

How can you tell if your finds are real gold, silver or diamonds? You can get a small acid test kit that will let you test a small portion of the item in question.

The acids are for testing different purities of metal. You will have to scratch a small portion of your jewelry on a small stone, and then place a drop of acid on the stone. If the metal residue dissolves, your item is not real. If it does not dissolve, congratulations on your find! Here is a good example.

The acid did not dissolve the gold. That means the gold is 14kt because I used a 14kt acid test kit!

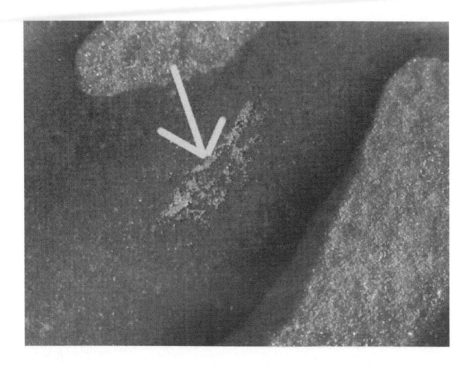

With diamonds it can be a little more difficult to spot a fake. The easiest way is with a diamond tester. These can get expensive, but they can be worth the investment if you are finding a lot of rings with stones in them.

If you don't have access to a diamond tester then a trustworthy jeweler will be able to tell you. **Don't ever let a jeweler leave the room with your prize, they just may try the old switcharoo and tell you it is a fake.**

If you have a loupe, you can usually spot a real diamond pretty easily. Diamonds will have small spots of carbon that you will be able to see in them. A really good diamond will have less carbon. These are the most expensive diamonds.

Selling Your Finds

At one point or another, you may want to actually sell some of that treasure that you have found. If you have a lot of gold, you may want to hold on to it. It will only increase in value, but if you have to part with some of your treasure, there are some right ways and some wrong ways to go about doing it.

First things first. Stay away from pawn shops. No offense to any pawn shop owners that may be reading this book. Pawn shops just don't pay full value on anything. If you need some cash in a hurry, then a pawn shop is your best bet. If you can wait a few days, then you can get twice or even three times what a pawn shop offers you.

Is it okay to sell your finds? This is up to you. You may feel morally obligated to find the original owner of an item that you have found. There is nothing wrong with this. I have returned several pieces of jewelry, but I have sold quite a few too. Selling off some of your finds is a great way to upgrade to some better equipment. A good metal detector does not come cheap, and you have worked hard for all of your treasure. There is nothing wrong with rewarding yourself.

You can sell just about any type of metal that you find. Of course you will be able to sell gold, silver and platinum, but many people forget that you can sell old lead fishing weights too. Those things are not cheap, and fisherman will gladly pay you for them. I have sold a lot of lead weights this way. Just think of it as recycling.

Selling some of your precious metals.
There are several ways to sell off some of your precious metal items. You can try to sell your treasure online through some of the popular websites, and there are plenty of people who make good money doing this. I prefer to sell my precious metal items to a refinery. They pay top dollar for gold, silver and platinum.

Some people won't use refineries because it involves sending all of your valuable precious metals through the mail. There is a good chance that your package full of gold will magically disappear. There is any easy way to avoid this. Never send it all in one batch. Plus, the US postal service offers insurance and signed proof of delivery. You make the call.

I have sold a lot of gold this way, and I have never had a problem. You simply securely send your gold, silver or platinum to the refinery and a week or two later, you get a nice check in the mail. Time to get that new metal detector that you have had your eyes on for months. This is one great thing about metal detecting. It is the only hobby that really does pay for itself. You may even be able to sell your treasure to a local jeweler that you have an arrangement with. This is a great way to get top dollar. Just make sure that the jeweler is someone you can trust.

I have used two refineries with no problems. Here is their contact information.

ARA
http://www.aragold.com/
1-800-216-9796
972-620-6020
2431 Walnut Ridge St.
Dallas, TX 75229

Midwest Refineries
1-800-356-2955
4471 Forest Ave.
Waterford, Michigan 48328

Metal Detecting With Kids

Metal detecting with kids can either go really well, or it can go really bad. Kids will love the idea of digging up treasure with you, but after they dig up a couple of less than stellar finds, kids may want to head back to the car. Their short attention span can quickly turn what you thought would be a great day into a quick trip home.

If you are going to be taking a young one with you, you may want to level the playing field a little bit. Bury some objects that they will think is treasure, and lead them to it. This will keep them from getting bored, and it may get them hooked on metal detecting.

This is how I got my son to really enjoy metal detecting. Now he rarely wants to miss a good day hunting for treasure. I have found three really good finds with my son, and these three moments created memories for both of us that will last a lifetime, and they all happened within months of each other.

Shells On The Beach

When my son goes metal detecting with me, he likes to do all of the digging. He demands it now, so I let him do all of the work.

I have been teaching him how to use the scoop, and how to identify and find items in that scoop of sand. You may not believe this, but sometimes it can be hard to see your treasure in that small amount of sand. Coins like to stay hidden, and they are harder to see to the untrained eye.

I decided to take my son on a real adventure. He loves to explore, so I asked him if he wanted to metal detect an old island, one that had most likely never been detected. He only had one thing to say, "When?"

We left that day. We had to take a boat to get to the island, and at the front of the island was a small exposed beach. This would be the place to check first. People frequent the island, and they are always right on this small strip of beach.

We hit the beach and started getting signals immediately. They were only 1-2 feet apart, and some were within inches of each other. We were finding a lot of fishing tackle, and a lot of older clad coins. We were also finding some really interesting things that we could not identify. Small discs that looked like they could be really old coins.

We both glanced at these things, threw them in our stash, and kept hunting. It had already been a couple of hours, and we were almost done with this tiny stretch of beach. It was hard to believe that two hours had already gone by.

I got a big signal, and I mean big as in size. It sounded like a can. It was too big to be anything else. I told my son, "Hey, there is a big target here, but I would just leave it. It is a can."

He grabbed the scoop, and started digging. I shook my head and started searching the beach again. A few seconds later I hear him scream. It was a good scream. I turn around he yells dad, "It is a huge sniper bullet." In his hands was a never fired .50 caliber round. It was huge, and I thought to myself, "Could he have possibly fired this thing if he hit it with the scoop just right?" I suddenly did not want him to dig any more targets.

He was holding was a very old .50 caliber bullet, and he was thrilled. He looked at me and said, "Good thing I decided to dig up that can, huh dad?" Smart-ass! This was one of mine, and one of his best finds. Here is a picture of that old shell.

My oldest coin to date was found with my son as well. We were metal detecting in an area that has a lot of history. People have been using this specific beach area since the early 1800s, and this beach always produces something interesting. It is the same beach where I found all of those quarters at one time.

This beach is not hunted very hard by other metal detectorists. It is loaded with large and small pieces of iron. It is everywhere, and it makes it very difficult to hunt. Like I said, I have had some really good luck there in the past. This was the first time that I took my son. I told him how there were iron targets everywhere. He just wanted to do some digging.

We hit the beach, and like I said, there were iron targets all over the place. I know from past experience that the iron thins out the further out in the water you get. I could only imagine how many good targets are buried deep under all of the iron targets. The iron targets are huge too. I am not talking about a lot of bobby pins. There are huge iron beams and segments of beams all over the place.

Our first good target was a penny. Whoo hoo! As we started to make our way out into the water, I got a good shallow signal. My son dug it up and out pops a small black coin. From the size of it, I tell my son that it is a dime. He rubs it with his fingers and says, "It says one dime on the back, but it looks weird."

He hands me the coin, and I look at it. It does look odd, but it is covered in a thick black greasy like substance. This is what happens to Silver in the salt water. I can't really make out the date or any other details at the moment. I put the dime in my pocket, and we continued our hunt for treasure never finding much else.

When we got home, we were both anxious to take a closer look at our mystery dime. I put a small amount of toothpaste on the coin and rubbed it in. This helped remove most of the black greasy like substance. I could clearly see the date. It said 1853. This was by far the oldest coin that I have found on a beach. Think how long that dime has been out there. I have hunted that same exact spot several times, but that dime was not there then, or it was beyond the reach of my metal detector. Yet another great memory for both my son and I. The old dime is now part of his coin collection.

Here is a picture.

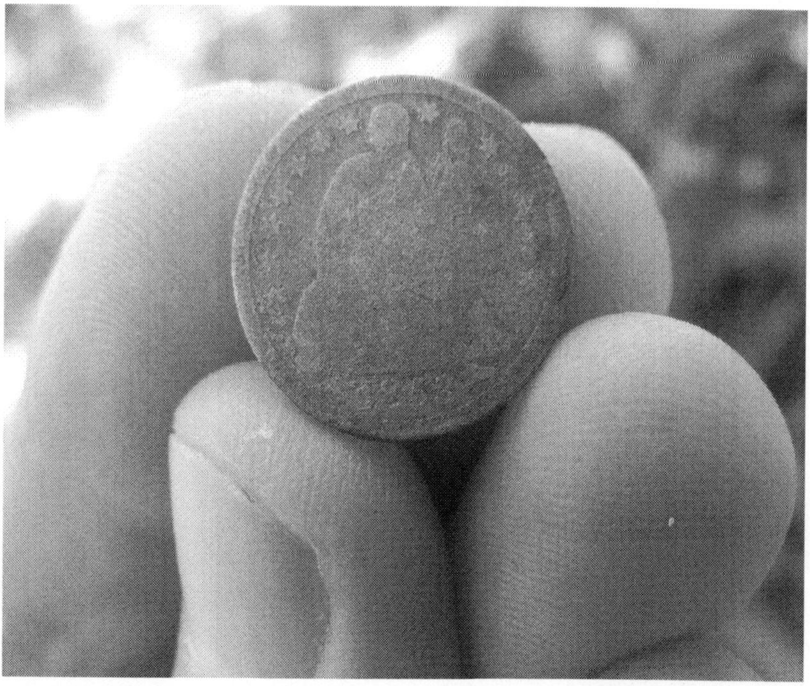

The first time my son found a ring on the beach was a really good experience for both of us. It happened right after Memorial Day. As you can probably guess, Memorial Day is a very busy beach holiday. I know from past experiences that this holiday almost always coughs up some really nice treasure.

We waited until Monday afternoon to start our hunt. The tide was perfect. It would be low tide at 7:00 P.M. This meant that we would be able to hunt in the later part of the day. It would be nice and comfortable, but I was wrong. For whatever reason, there was no breeze that day and the beach was hot.

It is really easy to get excited and forget about how far you have walked down the beach. This might not sound like a bad thing, but you have to walk all the way back. This was one of those days.

My son and I had walked for a very long time. We were enjoying the scenery. What teenage boy is not going to like walking down the beach. He had a hard time keeping his eyes in his head.

The bad news was that we were not finding anything. We had maybe a dollar in change and we had been hunting for almost three hours. That is just how things work sometimes.

I could tell my son was really frustrated as we walked

down the beach. We were almost to the car when I got a nice signal from my metal detector. My son was right on the spot with the scoop. This would most likely be the last target of the day.

He scooped some sand and I swung the coil over the hole. No more signal. He had it in the scoop. He rinsed the sand out of the scoop in the water and I saw his eyes light up. He opened his mouth and very loudly said, "Holy crap! It is a huge...." I quickly put my hand over his mouth and gave him the universal sign for be quiet.

He looked at me puzzled. I quietly asked him what was in the scoop. He quietly said, "It is a huge ring." I said, "Slip it into your pocket, and be quiet." There were still people all over the beach.

You may wonder why I did this. I am not trying to be dishonest. I am not trying to take anything from anyone, but there are people who will jump at the opportunity to claim something that is not theirs. I have been there and done that. I have said this before. DO NOT ANNOUNCE THAT YOU HAVE JUST FOUND A RING! You will get the attention of everyone on the beach, including the dishonest people who will lie and say that it is theirs. Just put your find in your pocket and go on your way.

When we got back to the car, my son pulled a big shiny ring out of his pocket. It was dark in the car, but I could tell that it was a really good find because it was very heavy. It turned out to be a platinum and gold band. How would you like this to be the first ring you find on the beach? There is a picture on the next page.

Research Really Pays Off!

There is nothing wrong with just free strolling down the beach looking for treasure with your metal detector, but if you can do some research and take a look into the past, you may be greatly rewarded.

You can begin your research at a local museum or a local library. The object of this type of research is to learn as much as you can about the history of a city, so that you will have some good places to hunt. Hunting old forgotten areas of the past can prove to have great payoffs.

You can look for maps or any historical pictures of the area. A lot can change in a short amount of time, and if you are at a local museum ask questions.

We also have this wonderful thing called the internet. It is loaded with historical data, but most people never use this data. I have found some excellent leads on the internet that turned out to be good places to hunt. Try to find places where people gathered around the water in the past. This is where you will find some great relics.

Start talking to some locals. I have been told my a few different old timers where a chest of gold coins is located a few miles out in the surf. These two individuals both told me what section of the beach these coins have been found on. I have yet to find one, but I keep looking.

I had another older gentleman tell me where an old casino use to exist in the early 1900s. I had no idea that there was a casino at this location, and none of the historical data that I had seen in the past mentioned it. I thought it was interesting, and worth a try. He told me that the casino was full of nickel slot machines. On my first trip to this area, I found two Indian head nickels in the surf. What he told me was true.

Research is really important, and it can lead to some really great finds.

The Changing Tides

The tide will have one of the largest influences on the way you hunt. There are two basic tides, high and low. You probably already know this, but there are certain times when high tide may be higher, and low tide may be lower. It all has to do with seasons and the Moon. If you can hunt what they call a negative tide, then you will get a chance to hunt some areas that are usually underwater.

Study the local tides for the area that you are going to hunt. It never hurts to see where everyone is on a particular day. If the tide is high for the majority of the day, then when the tide goes out, you will be able to find good targets all over the beach.

If the tide is low for most of the day, then you will find most of your good items at the low tide line, but the tides can have other affects on the beach, and the way you hunt.

When the tide comes in, it pushes a lot of things up with it. It also tends to bury heavier objects. The moving water is what makes the items move on the beach. The deeper the water is, the less an item will move. If the area is constantly being battered by waves, those waves will push items towards the high tide line. I have found plenty of gold rings in this area. Other treasure hunters swear by the low tide line, but you can find good targets everywhere in between.

In my experience it has worked like this. The high tide line will produce everything. If you are hunting in the high tide line, you can expect to find rings, coins, trash and everything else. Hunting the low tide line always equals fewer finds for me, but more quality finds.

Tides can change with the seasons too. Certain times of the year will produce different tides, but it all really depends on where you live. Each beach is different, and each beach is effected differently by the tides.

The tides move more than water too. The whole beach is moving all the time. The sand that the kids are playing in today, can be a mile down the beach a week later. Here is the perfect example.

I found a class ring, and on the inside was an inscription. I was able to locate the original owner, and return the ring. He told me where he lost the ring and when. I found the ring about 2 miles from where he had lost it, and I found it about two months after he lost it. The sand is always moving. It is just moving too slow to notice in a short period of time. Landmarks on the beach can give you clues. Poles, signs or trees in the sand will be able to give you some good signs on what the sand is doing.

On some beaches you will find nothing but mushy sand at the low tide line. Heavy objects will sink quickly in this mushy sand, and there are a lot of people who won't hunt the mushy sand, but I have found some good rings in that mushy sand, so I don't pass it up. I basically take whatever type of conditions the beach wants to throw at me, and hunt accordingly.

If I can't get out on an outgoing tide, then I will hunt the high tide. For me, it is just fun hunting. If you can get out for the low tide, it is a great idea to get to your spot two hours before low tide. This will give you two hours to hunt the outgoing tide. You will be able to get to those prime areas where moms and dads seem to lose all of their jewelry.

Can you really find rings on the beach?

A lot of people don't believe that you can actually find rings and other jewelry on the beach, but you can. My dad once told me that he did not understand how someone could lose a ring. It is really easy actually.

The beach is one of those magical places where people forget about the world for a little while. They get to enjoy the sun, sand and surf, and they completely forget about any jewelery that they may be wearing.

To protect themselves from the harmful rays of the sun, they load up on the sunblock. Sunblock is slippery. It makes rings slide right off.

When people are at the beach, they are usually doing one of two things. They are either sleeping in the sun, or playing. They may be playing out in the water. The cooler water makes your skin shrink. When your skin shrinks, your rings fall right off, and you never even realize until you get back home.

There are also a lot of people playing sports. They may be throwing a ball, a frisbee, or they may be casting a fishing pole. All three of these are great ways to lose a ring, especially if you are wearing sunblock.

There is another way that people lose jewelry on the beach,

playing in the sand. Digging in the sand, making sand castles and getting buried are all great ways to lose your jewelery.

What about the waves. Do you think the waves could knock a ring off of a hand that has somewhat shrunk as a result of the cooler water? Doesn't the sunblock just make it all that much easier?

This is how and why people lose their jewelry on the beach. Just about everything that people do at the beach can aid in losing their jewelry.

The Weather Can Wreak Havoc On The Beach

Before I mention anything about the weather, remember this. Safety first. If it is too dangerous to go outside because of the weather, then don't go. The beach can be a very dangerous place during a serious storm. It only takes one small rogue wave to knock you over. Once you are down, the ocean will claim you as its own and drag you down to Davey Jone's Locker. The sea is merciless, don't become a victim. Stay inside until the storm has passed and the seas have calmed down.

The weather will always have the single most powerful effect on the beach. A hurricane or a tropical storm can be hundreds of miles away, but it will produce large and dangerous surf that can quickly remove a lot of sand from a beach. A beach can be instantly transformed into a treasure chest, and it can also quickly go back to the way that it was.

You don't have to wait for a hurricane, or a tropical storm to come blowing through either. There are plenty of times when a good old thunderstorm can transform the beach. You also have seasonal weather to think about too. Cold fronts that come barreling down from the North can quickly move a lot of sand off the beach. It is up to you to be there and get all of the treasures. That brings me to my next topic...

The Seasons

No matter what beach you plan on hunting, chances are really good that it has seasonal influences, and these influences can be much more than weather. Think about the times of the year when the beaches are the busiest.

Spring Break is usually the start of it, and then when Summer rolls around, the beaches are packed. These make for some great seasonal hunting. You may find that you have better luck in the Summer when there are more people at the beach, but you may also find that with the change of seasons comes a change in the beach.

Here is how it works on the beach that I like to hunt. For most of the year, the wind is either out of the East, the Southeast, or the South. The wind and waves both come from these directions for most of the year. These conditions naturally push sand up on the beach. It builds up quickly. When Winter rolls around everything changes real fast.

Suddenly the wind is now out of the Northeast, and with it the waves start coming out of the Northeast too. When a cold front comes through, the waves get big and nasty, and the combination of that change of wind and wave direction can remove all of the sand that built up all Summer in just a few short days.

Being there when this happens can quickly fill your pocket

with all sorts of treasures. It is not unusual to run out of steam before you run out of targets. Digging 500 holes in a short amount of time is tiring, even when you are finding good stuff. These pictures below illustrate the perfect example of a good seasonal change.

Before the seasonal winds and waves hit. Notice a nice flat beach. There is a gradual angle as you get towards the water.

Here is the very same beach the next day. A strong
Northeast wind came in over night and removed about
three feet of sand.

A Big Ring and A UFO

When Summer rolls around, I prefer to hunt right before the sun goes down and continue after the sun has set. It can be exhilarating to be on the beach on a clear Summer night. A nice breeze to keep things cool, and plenty of things to dig up in the dark.

I remember one evening in the middle of the Summer when two strange things happened to me. I was walking North along the beach and my plan was to hunt where everyone had parked on my way up the beach, and then when I turned to come back, I would work the low tide line. According the the local weather reports, it was going to be a perfect night.

By the time I was half way through my hunt, I had already found two nice gold rings where people had been parking their cars. I was in great spirits and the sun was setting. Soon I would have the beach to myself. The sun went down, and the stars lit the sky. It was beautiful. I was getting tired so I decided it was time to turn and head back. I could hit the low tide zone and keep my feet wet.

I approached the low tide line eagerly, and that's when I saw it. It was a shooting star. I was lucky to see such a good one, and then out of the corner of my eye, it flew back up into the sky. What the heck was that? I have never seen anything like it. There it was again and this time it fell again just below the horizon, and a few seconds later it rose back out of sight. I was baffled, but It looked like I was getting closer to this mysterious object in the night sky.

It would fall out the sky and then shoot back up like a rocket. It was just barely visible. I was watching the sky, and suddenly my metal detector made a sound that I loved to hear. It was a nice tone that 4 out of ten times meant gold was buried under my coil. I dug a quick scoop and looked over my shoulder and the UFO was still doing its crazy dance through the sky.

I threw the scoop of sand on the dry beach and moved my coil over the hole I had just dug. No more target. I had retrieved it in that scoop of sand. It was dark, and I had to feel my way through the pile of sand. I stuck my hand in the sand pile and a ring slid right around my finger. I laughed out loud.

I pulled my hand out of the sand pile and reached down with my other hand to try and feel the ring that was around my finger. I could not see anything. My thumb brushed the top of the ring, and my heart raced. There was a huge setting on top of the ring. If this thing was a diamond, it was a big one.

I don't carry a light with me when I hunt at night, but I do carry a cell phone. I quickly fumbled for my cell phone so that I could shed some light on my recent find.

The light that came from the cell phone was just enough light to tease me even more. I was still a good distance from my car. I kept the ring on my finger, and looked back at the UFO. It was still there. I started to walk faster towards where I had parked my car. As I got closer to my car, I got closer to the UFO. It was not that far out there. I squinted to try and make sense of it, and then it hit me. It was a kite. I could see the kite string in the moonlight. I followed the string to a gazebo on the beach. Someone had tied this kite to the top of the gazebo and it was flying up and down all on its own. For a while it had me stumped.

When I got home, I told my wife, "I think I found a huge diamond ring." Her response was, "Let me see it." I held out my hand, and she slid the ring off my pinky finger.

I could see it in the light, and it was huge! I handed her the loop so she could look for any markings. There was a 14k stamp on the inside of the ring. A quick acid test told us that the ring was real 14k gold, but what about the diamond? I did not have a diamond tester, so I would have to wait until morning to take it to a professional who instantly verified that it was indeed a real diamond. It was just over 1 carat in size. How would you like to find something like this?

Reading The Beach

Learning how to read the beach can be a huge help when you are metal detecting, and it is not that hard to do in most cases. If the beach that you are hunting looks like a large flat piece of slate, then hunting will be tough, and the beach will be impossible to read. Finding anything that is old will most likely not happen. You may be able to find some fresh drops though.

Reading the beach is basically looking for areas on the beach where things might have accumulated. The first thing that I do every time I go to a beach to detect is this.

I will stand at the highest point on the beach, and slowly examine the beach in both directions. What am I looking for? I am looking for holes, pockets or spots that look like sand has been removed. You can see them best from a higher point on the beach. I have mentioned some of them already.

There may be scallops or low laying areas that can bee seen from a distance. If there are, these are the places where I will start hunting first. If they are in the distance, then that is where I am headed.

On certain beaches you may also notice sloughs or small deeper channels that run parallel to the beach. These little sloughs are where a lot of people play, and they are also a good place to hunt. With all of that sand removed, you will be able to get your metal detector coil 4-5 feet deeper than you would normally. These little sloughs can be great places to start your hunt, and they should be a beacon that draws you in. Hit any deep holes that you can spot on the beach, or in the surf first. These will produce your best chance of finding gold, and other heavy metals.

Gold is funny on the beach. Heavier gold items like rings will quickly sink on most beaches. If the sand is really soft and mushy, then the gold rings will sink fast. If the sand is hard and compact, then it will take them a much longer time to sink to the hard under layer.

If you were able to dig really deep at a beach you would find that the deeper you go, the more compact and hard the bottom will get. You may even eventually hit a layer of rock or coquina. Gold will settle down until it hits a surface that prevents it from sinking any further. It could be hard packed sand, rocks, a shell layer, or anything that prevents it from sinking.

Here is a good diagram that explains the different layers of the beach.

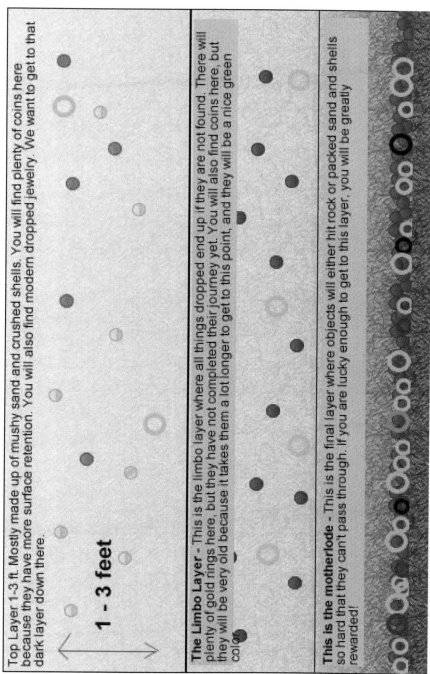

Top Layer 1-3 ft. Mostly made up of mushy sand and crushed shells. You will find plenty of coins here because they have more surface retention. You will also find modern dropped jewelry. We want to get to that dark layer down there.

1 - 3 feet

The Limbo Layer - This is the limbo layer where all things dropped end up if they are not found. There will plenty of gold rings here, but they have not completed their journey yet. You will also find coins here, but they will be very old because it takes them a lot longer to get to this point, and they will be a nice green color.

This is the motherlode - This is the final layer where objects will either hit rock or packed sand and shells so hard that they can't pass through. If you are lucky enough to get to this layer, you will be greatly rewarded!

This bottom layer is the layer that holds all of the gold and older coins. I have never had the chance to get to the very bottom layer yet. I have just not been fortunate enough to be in the right place at the right time. I have seen and spoken to one man who has. He showed me what he found in a few short hours when a freak storm removed almost all of the sand from his beach.

In just a few short hours he had found what most people find in a few years. He had over 50 gold rings, 80 silver rings, and enough old valuable coins to open a coin collection shop. The tide eventually pushed him out of his little honey hole. He went back the next day to the very same spot at low tide, and the hole had been filled with sand, and there were no targets to be found. It can happen that fast, so if you see a nice deep cut, scallop, or anything that looks good, don't hesitate, get your coil there as fast as you can. Once you are in the hole, slow down and reap your rewards.

Reading the beach is simple, but it may take you a little bit of time to get the hang of it. The simple concept is this. You are looking for low laying areas where sand has been recently removed by wind, waves, currents, tides or anything else. These are the places where you should start your search.

How To Hunt

Of course I have saved the best for last. In order to find more treasure on the beach, you will have to know what you are doing. The very first thing that you need to understand is this. Metal detecting is not a race. This is one time when slow and steady really does win the race.

Now you need to do is familiarize yourself with your metal detector. You will have to learn how to operate it, and that is beyond the realm of this book. There are too many different metal detectors out there.

There are a few things that might make your metal detector give you false signals. Waves moving over the coil are known to do this, uneven swings are known to do this, and bumping your coil into the ground can also cause your metal detector to produce false signals.

You may want to take some change with you on your first time out. Bury the change at different depths, and see how your metal detector works. You can do the same thing with some of your own jewelry. Tie a string to anything that you don't want to lose.

In order to maximize your finds you need to keep your coil as close to the ground as possible. This can take a little bit of time to master. When you swing the coil of your metal detector, you want the swing to be a nice even swing. Your metal detector should be the same distance from ground throughout the entire swing. A lot of people will swing their metal detector coil like a pendulum. This is a mistake, and you will be missing targets.

Keep the coil close to the ground, make nice even swings that don't raise in height as you go from left to right, and take your time. This is not a race.

Here are some examples of the right and wrong way to swing your coil.

The right way

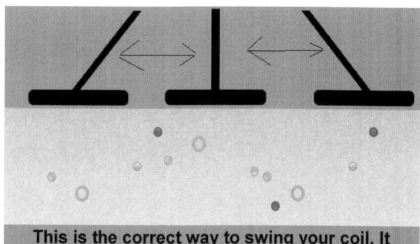

This is the correct way to swing your coil. It should be the same distance from the ground when you are furthest to the right and left

The WRONG way!

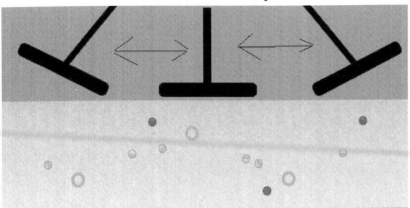

This is the wrong way to swing your coil. It can cause false signals and it puts the coil further from the targets.

Once you are ready to start swinging, you have to pick a place to start. If you can't seem to read the beach, or the beach is not giving you any clues, look at this drawing. This is how the beach is laid out where I like to hunt. You should focus all of your efforts where people have spent the most amount of time recently.

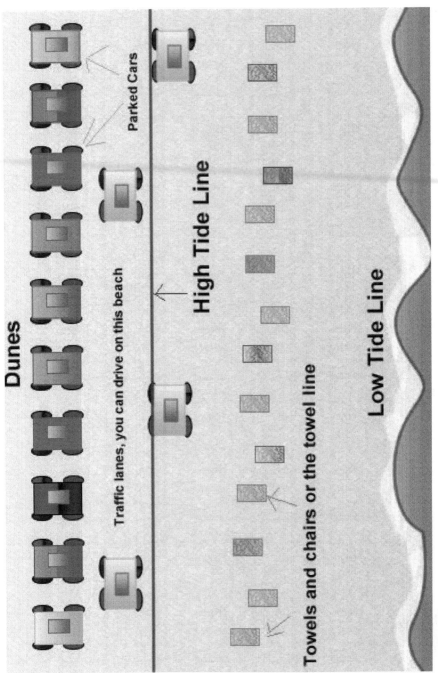

Dunes

Parked Cars

Traffic lanes, you can drive on this beach

High Tide Line

Towels and chairs or the towel line

Low Tide Line

If I can't see any deep spots on the beach, I start hunting in a pattern. I hunt in a big W shaped pattern to try and determine where the targets are on the beach. I drag my scoop to make a line that shows me where I have been. See the image below.

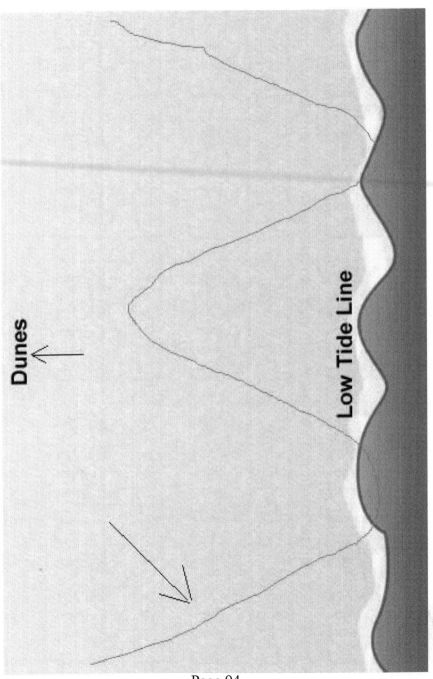

This is a great way to find out how things are being distributed on the beach. While I am doing this pattern, I look for more than one target in close proximity to each other. If I find a couple of targets that are really close to each other, it could be a very good sign that I have found what I have called a sticky spot.

When I find an area on the beach where there are multiple targets, I close my W pattern to a tight grid. See the image on the next page.

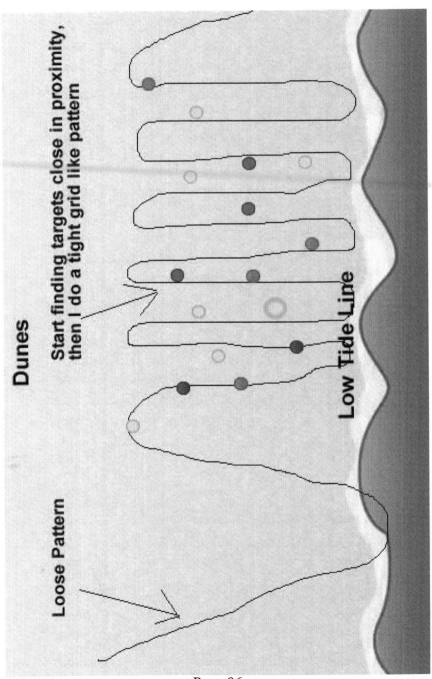

This tight grid allows me to get as many targets as I can find, and it works every single time.

If you are traveling a long distance between targets take a look back behind you, and try to see if you can see any sort of pattern to where you have been finding things. You may be able to find a coin line. See the image on the next page.

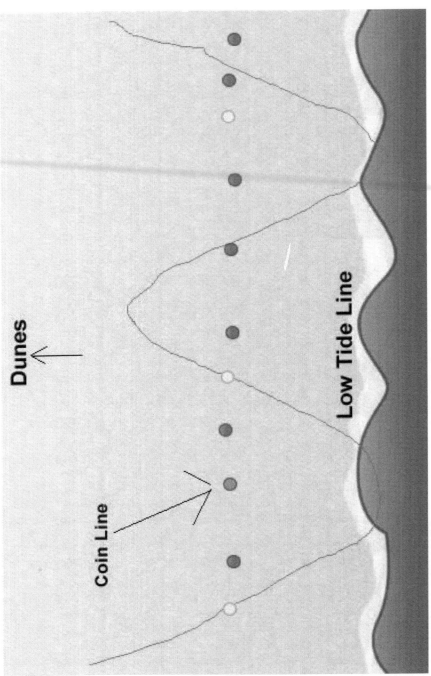

Metal detecting on the beach is not hard, and if you use these methods that I mentioned above, then you will find plenty of targets.

Pinpointing A Target

This can be one of the most difficult things to learn when you are new to metal detecting. Modern metal detectors are making it easier and easier to pinpoint a target, but I use a certain method. When I get a good signal, I move my coil back and forth over the area a little faster but with very short swings. I let my ears and eyes work together to tell me where the target is. I might spend 10-15 seconds doing this until I am certain I know exactly where the target is. Then it is time to dig. You might not get your target the first time. Here is how I do it.

After I have dug a scoop of sand, I move my coil back over the hole and listen for a sound. If I still hear the target in the hole, I empty my scoop and try again. I repeat this method until the hole that I have been digging does not produce a sound.

I should have my target in my scoop. I will then step away from the hole and sand that I have already dumped, and dump my scoop full of sand. I will try to flatten out the sand with the side of my foot. It makes it easier to scan the sand. If I don't see my target, I just move my coil over the spread out sand until I locate the target, and then I lightly kick that area of sand. Most of the times the target will reveal itself. I will also use my coil to separate the sand, and a lot of times I can move the target with just a little bit of sand with just my coil. This almost always reveals my target.

Digging Up Your Targets

Hopefully you took my advice and got the best scoop that you can afford. You will have to learn how to use your scoop, and with enough practice you will be able to retrieve your targets like a pro.

I can usually tell how deep a target is from the sound my metal detector is making. If it is just a faint sound, then it will be deep. If it is loud, then it will not be deep. It is pretty simple.

Shallow targets are really easy to get. You can usually get them with just one scoop. If you are in the water, you can just dunk your scoop in the water and sift all of the sand out leaving your target laying in the bottom of your scoop, unless your target was an earring. If it was, it will most likely fall through the holes in the scoop, and you will have to start your hunt all over again.

If you are digging in the wet sand, and your target is very deep, you may not be able to retrieve it. When you are digging in the wet sand, you have to dig really fast. The hole will start to cave in on itself, and when it does your target will sink even further. Keep trying. I have almost given up on several instances only to pull a really nice piece of jewelry out of the hole a second or two later.

As tempting as it may seem to get down there and shove

your hand in the soft sand to try and retrieve a target, don't do it. The one time that I had this bright idea, the target was half of an old beer can. You can only imagine how bad it cut my hand when I reached down into that soft sand and hit the razor sharp edge. I also heard a story once of a fellow who stuck his hand in a hole that he had been digging at the beach. He dug around in the sand, and then his hand found the target. His hand was wrapped around the barrel of a gun. Don't stick your hands in the sand. It is not worth the trouble.

There are also times when a target will disappear in the middle of digging. Sometimes it sinks deeper, but I have found that most of the times the target is still in the hole. I have noticed that the sand seems to somewhat amplify a deep target with my machine. I might remove 2-3 scoops of sand only to find no signal in any of the sand that I dug, and no signal in the hole either.

I have always found that the target is one or two more scoops down, and I almost always get it. There are times when I have had targets completely disappear, and I have to abandon the spot, and refill the hole. I even go so far as to widen the hole so I can stick the entire coil down in the hole to see if I can locate the target. This has worked for me on more than one occasion.

Hunting In The Water

Hunting in the water is a completely different experience. Everything may weigh less in the water, but metal detecting in the water is a lot harder. The water slows everything down. It becomes more difficult for you to move in the water, and it becomes more difficult to move your coil in the water. Some people find it too difficult and avoid it entirely. Safety is also an issue when you are hunting in the water, and it is a good idea to wear some sort of life preserver if you plan on hunting for any extended period of time in the water. It only takes one small wave to catch you off balance and send you down to the bottom where the current could easily drag you away.

You will find that digging targets in the water is difficult too. As soon as you remove a scoop full of sand, a wave will come and fill the hole back in. If the waves are getting the best of you, you may be better off turning your body sideways when the waves hit you. This will put less of your body in the way of the crashing wave and make it easier to withstand the abuse that the ocean is dishing out. When the water is rough, I try to stay out of it. Finding a gold ring is not worth drowning. You may want to do the same.

See You At The Beach!

If I could give you just one tip, it would have to be this. Persistence pays. It might be a while before you find your first gold ring, but what is most important is this, having a good time. You never know what you may dig up. You could dig up some ancient Roman coins, some real pirate treasure, some really old jewelry, old coins, modern technology, some toys, modern jewelry, meteors, raw gold or anything that is metal. There is a whole world of treasure buried just a few inches under the ground, and it is up to you to go dig it up! Good luck, have fun out there, and see you at the beach!

One Final Story

I will leave you with one more story that I think is pretty incredible.

One summer afternoon I was hunting a stretch of beach that I always hunt. The breeze was fresh and beautiful. It was a great day to be out there.

About half way into my hunt, I find a nice crucifix. I wipe the sand from the cross and toss it into my pocket. I was working a good area that was loaded with small change.

The path that I was taking was right towards two women that were enjoying the summer breeze. They were sitting in beach chairs, and each woman had their purse sitting at their feet.

One of the woman looked at me and said, "Finding any treasure?" I nodded and kept on going. The other woman got out of her chair and approached me. This is not unusual. I often get approached by people that are curious about metal detecting. I took off my headphones as she approached.

She looked at me and asked, "Do you ever find anything really good?"
"Sometimes." I said.

She asked me if I found anything good today. Usually

when someone asks me this, I just say no, but for some reason I felt I should show her the crucifix that I found.

I said, "I did find something pretty interesting." I was looking for the crucifix in my pocket. I fumbled with some coins, and then I located the crucifix and pulled it out.

I said, "I found this nice looking crucifix right back there." I pointed in the direction I had just come from.

The woman's face changed, and she turned and walked back to her chair. She started looking through her purse. She came back to me and said, "Can I see that." I handed her the crucifix, and she started to cry.

Now I was in what I would call a very awkward situation. The woman looked me in the face and then she wrapped her arms around me and started hugging me. Her friend approached us and said, "What is going on?"

Her friend exclaimed, "He found my cross. I did not even know it was gone. We were just down there 20 minutes ago and a wave came in with the tide. It knocked my bag over. My crucifix must have fallen out." She started to cry again.

Her friend looked at me and said, "You don't know how important that crucifix is to her. Her mother gave it to her right before she died. She takes it with her everywhere she goes."

I didn't know what to say or do, so I just kind of stood there for a moment. The woman stopped crying, hugged me again and said, "Thank you!"

I went on my way. I never found anything else that day, but that was an incredible experience!

Have fun out there!

7 Park st YO24 1BQ to 1st

1 A

5028151R10061

Printed in Great Britain
by Amazon.co.uk, Ltd.,
Marston Gate.